CONTENTS

WHEN THE WANDERERS COME HOME

African
POETRY
BOOK SERIES

Series editor: Kwame Dawes

WHEN THE WANDERERS COME HOME

Patricia Jabbeh Wesley

University of Nebraska Press / Lincoln and London

Acknowledgments for the use of copyrighted
material appear on page ix, which constitutes
an extension of the copyright page.

The African Poetry Series has been made possible
through the generosity of philanthropists
Laura and Robert F. X. Sillerman, whose
contributions have facilitated the establishment
and operation of the African Poetry Book Fund.

Library of Congress
Cataloging-in-Publication Data
Names: Wesley, Patricia Jabbeh, author.
Title: When the wanderers come
home / Patricia Jabbeh Wesley.
Description: Lincoln: University
of Nebraska Press, [2016]
Series: African poetry book series
Identifiers:
LCCN 2016003756 (print)
LCCN 2016008740 (ebook)
ISBN 9780803288577 (pbk.: alk. paper)
ISBN 9780803295018 (epub)
ISBN 9780803295025 (mobi)
ISBN 9780803295032 (pdf)
Classification:
LCC PS3573.E915 A6 2016 (print)
LCC PS3573.E915 (ebook)
DDC 811/.54—dc23
LC record available at
http://lccn.loc.gov/2016003756

Set in Garamond Premier by Rachel Gould.
Designed by N. Putens.

This book is dedicated to the memory of my father, Moses C. Jabbeh, Kwadi Chee, for a lifetime of inspiration, love, and guidance. You are the hero of my life. I celebrate you always.

We are characters now other than before
The war began, the stay-at-home unsettled
By taxes and rumor, the looter for office
And wares, fearful everyday the owners may return, . . ."
—John Pepper Clark Bekederemo

ACKNOWLEDGMENTS

Crab Orchard Review for "Losing Hair"

We Have Crossed Many Rivers: New Poetry from Africa for "When Monrovia Rises"

Black Renaissance Noire for "Finally, the Allergist," "Looters of War 2011," "When Monrovia Rises," "You Wouldn't Let Me Adopt My Dog: A Poem for Ade-Juah," "For My Children, Growing Up In America," and "Medellin from My Hotel Room Balcony"

Connotation Press for "If You Have Never Been Married," "I Want Everything," "Sometimes, I Close My Eyes"

Heart for "I Go Home"

Literary Orphans for "Sometimes, I Close My Eyes" and "In My Dream"

The Enchanting Verses: Literary Review, for "Loss" and "What Took Us to War"

RedLeaf Journal's African Diaspora Folio for "Send Me Some Black Clothes"

BOOK I

Coming Home

So I Stand Here

They say thresholds are meant to keep

the outsider out, the insider, in. Crickets
forever creeping along walls, along the edges

of things. You must first lift your right foot,
and then the left, and then enter the hut

before the kola nut is served, before
the spiced pepper is offered, and the water

from the stream, handed to you. This is
the way of things, the way of life, clay to clay,

your hand holds not just a cup of water,
but the source of life. Tradition. After that,

the outsider is now an insider, but everywhere
I go, my country people have become

a different people. So, I stand here,
an outsider, at the doorpost. Do not tell me

that these corrugated old dusty roads
have emerged of themselves out of the war.

Or that the new songs these strangers sing
in this now strange country of ours are

from the time before the bullets. Do not tell
me that the kola nut you served me

will answer all of the questions that linger
in my soul. Do not tell me that I belong

to this new people. I have wandered away
too long, my kinsmen. I have wandered so far,

my feet no longer know how to walk the old
paths we used to walk. I do not know these

people, birthed from the night's passing
of lost ghosts. I do not know these people

who have so sadly emerged out of the womb
of war after the termite's feasting.

My kola nut has lost its taste, and the spiced
pepper, now, with a new spice. I am too

impure to meet my ancestors, and the gourd
of water I have just fetched from Ngalun

weighs heavily upon my head. I stand
at the threshold, my kinsmen, come and help

me over the doorpost that the termites
have eaten. I do not have the hands to greet

my ancestors. I do not have the hands
to greet my kinswomen, and the hand with

which I take hold of the kola nut is shriveled
by travel. The kola nut you served me

is no longer bitter, oh come, my kinswomen,
the horn blower has lost his voice. But they

tell me that the horn blower does not need
his voice to blow the horn to let me in.

What Took Us to War

Every so often, you find
a piece of furniture, an old head wrap
or something like a skirt
held together by a rusty pin.
Our years, spilled all over the ruggedness
of this war-torn place,
our years, wasted like grains of rice.

Relics of your past, left for you,
in case you returned accidentally
or intentionally, in case you did not
perish with everyone else.
Something hanging onto thread,
holding onto the years
to be picked up, after locusts
and termites have had their say,
the graciousness of looters,

the graciousness of termites
and temporary owners of a home
you built during your youth,
during the Samuel Doe years
when finding food was your life goal.
How gracious, the war years,
how gracious, the warlords,
their fiery tongues and missiles.

All the massacres we denied,
and here we are today, coming upon
a woodwork of pieces of decayed
people that are not really pieces

of woodwork at all.
This should be an antique, a piece
of the past that refused to die.

Wood does not easily rot, but here,
termites have taken over Congo Town
the way Charles Taylor claimed the place,
the way Charles Taylor claimed
our land and the hearts of hurting people,
the way the Atlantic in its wild roaming
has eaten its way into town
even as we roamed, in search of refuge,

the way whole buildings have crumbled
into the sea, the way the years
have collapsed upon years.
What took us to war has again begun,
and what took us to war
has opened its wide mouth
again to confuse us.
What took us to war, oh, my people!

Erecting Stones

JANUARY 2013

Here, in Congo Town, I'm picking up debris
from twenty years ago. Some remnants of bombs

and missile splinters, old pieces of shells from
the unknown past. A man strays into my yard,

wanting my old range and a fridge some wartime
squatters, passing through my home, did not take

away these twenty-two years, while my home floated
like a leaf, through the hands of mere strangers.

He will build coal grills for sale, but it is in the trash
that I'm searching for the past, searching for myself

in the debris of years past, and here, the upper
part of a cotton skirt suit, checkerboard fabric, black

and beige, size six, yes, that's me, those many years
ago, size six, high cheekbones, slender, sharp,

the losses we must gather from only memory.
But we're among the lucky, I tell myself as a former

neighbor stares at me, the new neighborhood
children, hollering around us. "I hear you're back,"

my once lost neighbor says, staring in awe that after
so long, we're still alive. "No, we're not," I say.

"We're only picking up the broken pieces of the years,
erecting stones, so the future can live where we did not."

"Thank you, Mrs. Wesley, for coming back to us,"
he says. "We just buried Zayzay yesterday."

"You're still burying the dead, over twenty years, still
digging and shoveling, to bury the young and early dead.

This is a country of ghosts," I say, "a county of ghosts."

Looters of War

Monrovia 2011

The still ruined places of the past
of bullet walls and buildings, despite
the desperation
                              to put the past away.

If only we could put ourselves in boxes.
If only we could put away the deep scarred
places, where sores are so deep

they cling like something too malignant
for words. When my children come home,
              I should walk them through

this place of now eroded landscapes, once
owned by dead people.

The rain splashes away muddy puddles
and out in the swamps, even the frogs
wail like old village women in mourning.

The stay-at-home have gathered overnight
to steal our land. The old rocky hillsides,
              the sloping fields and endless
beaches, all, taken by looters.

Coming Home

A POEM FOR MT

When MT calls me at dawn,
I think it's about Mother's Day.
But this is not about Mother's Day,
I see. Instead, it is his car,
broken into by thieves for old screws,
a toolbox full of the tools
he needs to unscrew his own Africa,
an air filter, to filter the years of dust
and mite bites, to filter the dust
from termites, eating into
the wood of things after the war.

This boy was supposed to be African.

The fetus, I cuddled like precious
diamonds in my body after grad school,
my small body, holding on to hope
that my son would be his own Africa someday.
This child I carried home in my young
womb so he would not wander far
has returned to a place
we used to call home.

But war is not a friend of the living.
War is not your neighbor, coming
with a basket of cookies in welcome.
War is an alien monster,
and so we packed up house and fled
years ago from this place.

And now, this same child, welcoming
home the mother, who has become
the wanderer. This same child, pulling
boxes and springs, tools and shovels,
felling old, unnecessary trees,
pulling rocks so stones, fallen
two decades ago, can stand again.

It is my son, scrubbing and mending,
trying to undo the war we started,
the foreigner, returning to his lost
country, overrun by battle.
There is a pile of dust,
concrete as rust, concrete as dust
cannot know concrete.
There is the dust from the past,
eating away the present.

Our people say, God gave us sons
to hold the wood, burning, above our roofs,
to hold the town on its screws.
But we are but wanderers, I tell my son,
the land we owned will no longer own us.
The land we teamed
has become unleashed with scorpions
and termites, so here you are, my son,
meeting the termite,
the eater of all life.

So, here you are, my son,
fighting a new war,
digging up old termite hills.

Send Me Some Black Clothes

Elegy for my homecoming

Sweet sorrow of family reunions around
the dead; so I get dressed for another funeral.

But I'm almost ashamed to burden my friends
with news of another dead relative, as if I were

some storehouse of dead people, as if I could
earn a living, announcing news of my dead

or dying brothers and sisters. I returned home,
walking into a place of dead bodies here,

in Monrovia, only corpses, the same manner
in which I left decades ago, walking through

dead bodies of my people during the war.
Someone, please send me some black clothes.

Liberians are dying like earthworms after
a long rainy night, dying, the way centipedes

crawl out of a burning shed to die quietly.
They say, life has many zigzags, many humps.

They say, if you live long, you will see something.
Sehseh Juway, the woman, named after my *Iyeeh*,

of whom I sing in my poems, of whom I've
strung this Grebo word around verses, *Iyeeh's*

namesake has died, so Uncle Robert travels
five hundred miles of rugged terrain by road

and dust because, there's no room to make
excuses not to bury your sister. So, here I am,

lost daughter, come home for something else,
and I find myself standing among caskets.

Life has rotted away, the remains of lack, when
a country decides to rise up, not from the ankles,

but from the head as those at the ankles die
of lack, as if living in lack were a curse, I say,

send me Second-Mourning clothes to spread
along the footpaths so millipedes can crawl.

Send me some Second-Mourning clothes, my
people, please, Liberia smells again of corpses.

The poor are burying their dead, so let the rivers
swell in rage. Let drums cry dirges against

the wind. Let mutiny break out upon the town.
There is too much death in town, so, I ask for

the town crier, he, too is dead. Ask for the horn
blower, he, too is dead. Ask for the *Bodior*,

the *Bodior*, too, is dead. Ask for the young virgins
and their suitors that used to line the roads,

they are all dead. Someone, please holler for me.
Someone, please send me some black *lappas*

to cover the ground in the Harmattan dew.

I Need Two Bodies

One, to sleep and the other,
to shuffle, push, and grind up the day.
One, to bend a rod,
and set the world upright,
the other, to cuddle the earth
so it holds on to its hold.

One, to inhale, and the other, to exhale.
One, to lie down upon freshly dewed grass,
the orange-red sun, dying down slowly
in my other body's eye.

I want my other body to drive like
a stubborn engine as stubborn
as a woman, after middle age,
my other body, standing on metal legs,
ready to grind
a large day downhill.
To empty these muscles of aching
pains down some drain.

I want my working body to sigh
and stand firm to all the battles
a woman must wage
against the grind of unsuspecting
roadblocks. One body, to be

the everlasting pull against push,
my one body, unbridled; legs,
as concrete as the Statue of Liberty
on a cloudy morning,

her gazing eyes upon
my old tired face as I sit
on a far ferry into the city
quiet, as sleep.

Then, my sleeping, eating,
resting body, rising out of unnecessary
things, tells this old one, "Be still,
be still and know that I am you.
Be still, and know
that I am Woman."

The Creation

Woman was made so clothes would have something
to wear. So shoes would find company, hair,

finely braided, hanging down the shoulders of an
unloose woman. A tightly fitted skirt, finding knees.

Some *lappa* suit, carved out of unyielding things.
Stiff fingers, sewing and sewing, until fabric

attaches itself to permanent skin. All the lost hours
and lost sleep, just so fabric can find sliding ground

on the back of a woman, feeding herself on scraps
of unwanted love in a city, long lost to map builders.

Woman was made so pavement would have feet
to carry. Loads of sharp heels, bare, only to shoes.

So feet would know the forgetfulness that comes
with stepping, the forgetfulness of twisting not just

to the rhythm of new love. Woman was made
so men would have trouble to fall into. Like a ditch,

dug so deep, falling into it only creates deep scars
in an already scarred heart. Woman was made

so worry would have a place to lease, so the sun
would find moon, so moon would have daylight

to blame for its own disappearance, so worry
would burn down the throat of some lonely man.

Woman was made to put the world in places where
place cannot hold earth. Woman, carved crudely

out of the beauty of ugliness, out of scarred pieces
of pain. Beauty, out of all the broken parts of a broken

city, where the heart has forgotten how to mend.
Woman was built out of corrugated pieces of zinc,

just so the earth would rebuild, so pain would forget
how to be. Earth, finding erectness in the small,

bent, carved places, where the world has been so
long broken, there is no longer any unmaking.

Woman was made to remake other women into
other hard pieces of burnt clay. So the clothing

we wear could talk to other clothing we can't wear.
Woman was made from scarred tissues of metal,

from the firmness of a brick wall, iron pieces
standing up at last for something. So tears

would have a face to wear, so pain would have
something to carry around, so the earth would

find the heart to heal all the brokenness of ruin.
Woman was made to unmake a man the way

you unmake a face the way you undo, to rewind
the corrugated heart of a world, too long broken.

And You Tell Me This Is a Funeral?

Theater. The news comes in,
and from every town and village,
like chickens that have heard
of scraps in town, women and men pour
in upon the Death house.
Po-po wlee-oh, po-po-wlee-oh,

Theater. Women, their hair loose, they
come, shouting, screaming, wailing,
and from out of the wood of things,
dirges burst out upon the mourners, because,
somehow, the dirge-singing girls
have come out of their silence

where for years, they learned how to wail
for the passing of the renowned king,
for the passing of the father-in-law,
for the passing of the husband,
for the passing of the townswoman, the
mother of children, the mother of mothers,
who is now dead, *Iyeeh Kpala.*

The women are seated out in a huge row
on *The Mat*, feet, stretched out
as if they will be here on this *Mat*
for years. They wail, as if taking turns;
they wail, when another woman arrives
from far away, her dusty feet and her
hair, unkempt, just for this moment.

She throws off her luggage from
the heat of her head and falls flat
on *The Mat*, rolling, screaming,
wailing, her own dirge, like a folk song.
Now she's wailing about the heroic deeds
of the town, of the townsmen before us,
of the townsmen of the Clan,
the ones that gave birth to the now dead
king or man or husband.
She wails, as if this man were
the last man left on the earth.

The chorus of women are now all
singing dirges, all of them, like a choir
for the dead, their musical rhythm
and lyrics will bring tears to the eyes
of the coldest man in the world.
And now, the history of the town
is being told on the tiny string
of a Grebo dirge, an intricate

of dirges, telling of the wars they've
fought, the heroes, lost, the children
that did not come out of birth
chambers because of those wars,
and this hero, now dead, an even
greater one than the heroes
the epic dirges can recount.

Theater, before the casket even arrives
from wherever Grebo caskets come,
mind you, it will be two weeks

of mourning or even more, of eating
kola nuts, of chattering and grumbling,
and then the eldest son comes out,
screaming all the anger
he's built up for decades,

and the wives narrate in their own
anger, family feuds, unfolding itself
like a loose string, unrolling itself
before the mourning crowd.
Mind you, everyone says,
"*Nyon-ne-nu-neh-oh*," as if this taboo
had not been broken before many times.
"People don't do that—oh," they say
with all the poetic music
Grebo can carry on a single line.

Theater. "And you tell me, this is a funeral?"
The Klao people will lay out the dead
as if the dead were a specimen to behold,
as if the grave were not a journey,
as if this laying out was meant
to prepare the dead for a higher calling.
Mind you, this is not for the living.

Theater. This is a libation for the living-dead.

Loss

A Dirge for Thomas Wadeh Boah

Wadeh, when you were born, they named you Wadeh.
In Grebo, your name is "Sorrow." Wadeh, Junior, dead,
just four months after I discovered that you were

still alive out there in some faraway city in Nigeria.
Port Harcourt, oil city, the hot dusky sun, Harmattan.
This morning, news came that you have just died.

Emptiness. So I sit here at my computer, going over
photos of you. My Facebook page, holding onto
so many messages from you, jammed into my inbox,

messages, as if empowered by the urgency of a rushing
river, the river that you were. At home, we knew you
were the Wanderer. Wadeh, sorrow, pain, loss, always

in and out, between bordering towns, Cote d'Ivoire,
Guinea, coming and going, as if laying out the miles
between you, family and home was your life goal.

Two decades back. Home. Liberia, and my mind
unfolds the pounding urgency of war, bombs, flight,
the forever displaced people that we are. So you left

your children in a refugee camp somewhere in Guinea,
so far away from home, forever. Lost. And everyone
said, "Junior is dead." For how else could we explain

this abandonment of children and wife? We held on

to the emptiness of losing you as ghosts hold on to us,
burying you in our minds. But it is not the losing

that makes emptiness a hollow, a space in an endless
place, as if digging and digging to find gold or to define
gold, or in the finding of gold, you discover that gold

is only rust or not just rust, but loss. Loss, when the war
took you so far away from us, like a leaf, blown away,
and then, like a ghost, there you were again.

So we thought we had truly found you. Now they tell
us that your dead, burnt body cannot be claimed.
That the one who has moved on into the other world,

where so many years ago, your father journeyed,
where our fathers roam free of borders and country.
They say there was fire, so we cannot even gather

your burnt body, your light-light-skinned body that so
reminded us of Bai Hne, our great father, the remnants
of what the war could not consume, lost people, lost

dreams, the new people without a country. But how do
we accept this news without beholding your body?
What we do not see remains alive forever in the eye.

I'd like to keep you the way you were; 1989, walking,
half-running into my yard, Monrovia, that standstill calm
before the war, before the rebels took the city from us.

I wanted to keep you so I could retrieve you forever,
Wadeh, firstborn, named after your father, Sorrow.
I'd like to keep you always, the way only the heart can.

If You Have Never Been Married

I guess I'm the saltshaker you always
wanted, the hot, spicy pepper,
the one, who can undo done things,

the troublemaker you saw in your dream.
When I tell you to wade the water
so the fish can swim upstream,

know that this is not the farm your father
left you. I guess, if you had me
in your home, your neighbors would

have smelled burning flesh long ago.
I guess, when the *lappa's* on fire,
it is the owner that's on fire.

I am not an art piece you can put up
on a wall. I guess I was born
upside down, oh, I mean upright.

Isn't everyone supposed to be born upside
down? How come each time a child
decides to be born standing up,

the midwife panics? This is what's wrong
with the world. Everything that's wrong
is right and what's right is wrong.

I guess, my uncle was right. "If you've never
been married," my *Borbor* used to say,
"you haven't seen anything yet.

Becoming Ghost

For the women telling me their war stories

My friends tell me that every photo I take
is a different person. As if each individual pose,

every bit of every effort by a photographer
has refused to see the same person twice.

As if a changing person were inside the single
person, as if I were a new personality of itself

outside of itself each time. So I stare at photos
taken at the same moment, same poses, same

suit, same red-framed glasses against jawline.
I sit still to see how the same woman can occupy

so many spaces and spirits, power to power,
spirit against spirit, as if an outside spirit were

to inhabit her being. As if I have been taken over
by many wailing women on their way to their

executions, on their way to mutilation, the power
of rape, so powerless. And the execution

of women, which, in itself leaves the war-ravished
warrior mutilated inside out, the emptiness

of ruined spaces, where a rebel never knows
when to end rebellion. As if I were being occupied

by the empty arms of those women, led away
from us, in line, their screaming infants, tossed

aside like dirt, or dashed against a wall that
knows not how to swallow blood, being asked

to swallow blood, the untold stories of unknown
women, walking, barefoot, drowned, after rape.

As if rape were not in itself an abomination.
I have become all the stories I've jammed into

the small spaces of a digital world of flash cards
and drives, too minute to hold up history

in its flat brain. A woman, half seated on a chair,
staring into the small space of my camcorder

lens, as if afraid of both the camera and the story
she will empty into the camcorder. As if, afraid

to own the chair and the story being held up
by the four frail legs of the chair. It is 2011,

and I'm still collecting Liberian women's war
stories that otherwise are dying. The victim, who

dies twice with the story, dying a hundred times.
As if I were the mind of many ghosts, collecting

ghosts stories, the mind that discovers more bones
at the burial site of old human skulls and bones,

we came here to forget. The room, full of women
who have come like an army of women to tell their

stories, are in tears now. I leave the room so they
do not see my own tears. There will never be

tissues sufficient to drown the cries of so many ills.
The woman stares into my camcorder as I return

to stand beside her while the camcorder rolls
in the hands of my assistant at the other end.

This camcorder may now know how to wail
silently in each telling. And then, the woman

drops her own bomb just like all the other women.
Oh, how each one of us carries between our

breasts, stories no one will believe. You can never
be the same after this sort of story-collecting

session, I tell you. To ask a woman to hold down
the legs of her younger brother, to hold him

in place, to calm his fighting legs and body
as rebels shave off his head is to ask her to die

forever inside out. Is to ask her to move her body
inside the body of another woman, is to ask her

to live a life of dying again and again. To ask her
to hold down her mother's last son, the same legs

she held, to change his diapers, her mother, looking
on so long ago to see how a girl becomes woman,

not knowing there was a future somewhere, so
heartless, where her girl child would become

woman through rape, through an abomination
of the sort that kills a nation, where sacrifice asks

too much of the sacrificial lamb. I am inhabiting
so many women's bodies. I am inhabiting living

ghosts, my people. I am becoming a body of water
as if my own tears were not sufficient for my one life.

As if all the tears of this nation could purify a land
so stained, it has become too impure for redemption.

As if this body of mine were sufficient in itself
to carry my own near-death stories, as if I have

become a new ghost, occupied by many other ghosts.
As if I have stopped being so the dead will live.

The Killed Ones

They will not allow themselves to go away.
The dead are not really dead,
we were told.
This is Africa, a land where ancestors send
their spirits to roam, to plow dark waters,
to keep the villages upon muddy ground,
where the fathers revisit the fathers.

The killed ones were not all renowned.
Not all birthed of royalty.
The killed ones are in the marketplaces,
some, without their heads. Some,
without their hearts; some without
their need to live.

The killed ones are not gone forever.
They return when the sun is setting upon
the creek, when the moon rests on
an ocean wave.
You do not kill the killed ones to keep
them away. This is a country of ghosts.

The Cities We Lost

After they left, rainy days came back
to find us
          among the ruins, in a city
resting on crutches.

There were the cliffs as if falling.

Old cliffs, old town, old villages,
the far wanderer, even the birds would
not stop looking.

The forgotten bones came alive, rising
on wings and black wandering feet,

then came looking,
          for those taken from among us,
for those of us left to fade into air.
On the road,

          a child was looking, sharp jaw
bones, tiny hands,
no need for crutches. The child had
become her own crutches of thin legs,
          no voice to carry away her legs,
no tears to open up her eyes to the sun,
as if she no longer needed voice.

But she thought I was her mother,
at the roadside.
          Maybe I was her mother,

sitting there, by the roadside.
And looking up at me
as if to follow this stranger that I was,
but how could I claim her

in the ruins that we had become?
        Amidst the bullets and rebels,
the suffocation of death
        and the dying,
death was more alive than us.

A City of Ghosts

for Monrovia

I have been taken over by ghosts,
a country and its litter of old bones,
forgotten and tossed away
by folks forgetting to remember.
I have been swallowed in the pages
where spirits cannot stop intruding
as I relive my own story
of living with ghosts.

I say, leave me alone; this is not your story.
As if I were on my way to the farm
after a dewed night has faded.
After the night has departed
and left the morning to keep
the remnants of the night's undoing,
as if to keep the wet of the night
so folks will remember
not to forget.

As if to keep the souls of those who left
and forgot to take their souls,
as if their coming and intruding
into the pages of my memoir
will bring them back.
They come, and they come
the way Grebo women come
when the King is dead, the way
they sit on *The Mat* to wail.

As if a farmer, in walking to his rice
field, forgot to pass or take the wetness
of the fresh dew from brush and petals
of wildflowers along the roadside.
As if ghosts had any reason
to haunt us, to follow us, to linger
in doorways, where memory
and time meet, where time is timeless
and we do not know it.

If I am haunted by ghosts,
If I am visited by all my weary mothers
and sisters and brothers, if I am visited
by friends who forgot to take themselves
when they left themselves,
then why are they not haunting
their murderers, those who carved them up
like pieces of logs,

those who shaved their heads away,
the way you shave hair from chin,
a piece of an oak's arm
from trunk? Those who broke them
into shreds of wood dust,
those, still walking and living,
who dug their unmarked graves?
Or are they really being haunted by ghosts,
real ghosts, living ghosts,
in their walking and talking?

July Rain

Today should be left for poetry.
Rain, as hard as stones, so the city
has folded like a snail.
Monrovia, what is it
you want from me now?
Not a poem. Not a story.
Already, all the poems I had
for you have been spilled
and left by a roadside
somewhere.

I laugh when my brother calls
to tell me that if the rain
should stop, he'll come to find me.
When my friend calls and says,
it is the rain that's keeping
her waiting to see me.

Here, legend tells the story
of the monkey who did not build
his house until the nightfall
of torrential rains.
Then from his branch, he promises,
"Tomorrow, when the rains stop
I will build me a house,"
until daylight, then again,
"Tomorrow, I promise,
when the rain stops,
I will build me a house."

I laugh that for centuries now,
people have used the rain
to flee, to run, not to do,
to suspend a marriage, to suspend
a divorce, to hold the baby
from coming out.

If the rain would stop, we
would stop making babies, they say;
if the rain should stop,
I will put my wife out
and find me a better one.
If the rain should stop,
I will run away from the man
that has beaten me all these
years, they say.

It is the rain, and it is pouring
down as if someone has
died and told the skies
to wail. But somewhere
in Africa, the sun is bright.
Somewhere, somewhere,
it is as bright as the sun,
and lovers are holding
hands, laughing.

I Go Home

I go home every night, barefoot, walking,
running. Sometimes, I'm driving my car,
and suddenly, the car is gone.
So I trample like a lost child,
the dark iron rocks of Monrovia, where
the word *corrugated* must have got its name.
Over the hills, where old gutters run
like small streams in between dilapidated
houses, jammed into one another
like the sheets of an old book,
soiled and spent, the way a woman is spent
by the unforgiving years of childbirth,

her breasts, flattened, the way you flatten
a sheet of dough for the oven. I go home,
where small, half-clothed children
run in between old, tin houses
of tarred, melting roofs. The children
and their make-believe war, their tiny feet,
pelting like rain, but I go home, holding on
to my long lost heart. Underneath
my blankets in my dream world,
it is after school or before school, the hot
Monrovian sun, melting greasy sweat
on the bare backs of children

who may never grow up, may never see
those teenage years, children, with fathers
and mothers, but parentless still.
I go, now my car is lost again and my
purse, also lost, and no one can say

how I got here from the smooth roads of my
too peaceful neighborhood, here in America,
where only a neighbor and her dog
may walk by, but I'm home.
Home, not to this decade, where I have
survived it all, the war and the torture
of hundreds of thousands, death

and near death; instead, I go home to the 1960s
of rugged Monrovia, almost virgin
and unspent, where I'm that small child,
running in between small houses
in Bishop Brooks, tomorrow's grease
on my bare back, Monrovia of the poor
who did not even know how poor they were,
did not even know how much of tomorrow
had been snatched away before dawn.
But somewhere in between the river
and the ocean, life is silenced.

I'm in my blue-and-white uniform now,
a high school teen again, with my own burdens
and fears without knowing I'd be so far away
today, I'd have to travel thousands of ocean
miles in my sleep to find my mother's grave
at a gravesite, now lost.
If your mother dies while you're on
a journey from home, in flight from bombs
and crumbling buildings, the fires
and the long line of starving refugees,
why should you also have to lose the grave
in which you safely laid her bones?

But I go home, where my father, so aged,
worries and worries, scared, his one child
is no longer there. Some days, my phone
rings and rings because somehow,
Pa has told my siblings that I'm ill and in bed.
So one by one, they call, wishing
I'd tell the truth, wishing I'd live long
enough to bury this old man I once
assured in his mother tongue, in promises
made from wet dewdrops.
The early dawn upon the green brush
of Tugbakeh. My Pa, who has lost the world

he built around himself with break walls,
a yard, so fenced in, it keeps the hot
blazing sun away and out,
so high, rebels marched through, carrying
guns and vengeance, leaving death behind.
I go home, again and again, where,
I do not have to seek the sun, but everywhere,
the world is so familiar, I do not need eyes.

Song for Mariam Makeba

November 9, 2008

On the radio in Monrovia, your voice, on a thin
string, in between the rushing wind, the sunshine.

You were always the dirge in the air, something
I wanted to cry for, that voice as if on an electric

wave, and I wished for a moment to touch your
hand, to sit on a sidewalk and cry with you.

I was seven or eight years old, always, my girl
eyes, wondering if I could see you someday.

I wanted to behold one of your musical notes
between all the crushes I carried in my small

heart, but I was only eight years old then, times
when Mama said eight-year-old girls couldn't

get married. There you were, inside that small
radio on Mama's table, and on every table

in the neighborhood, Bishop Brooks, that
crowded place with no space for a small child

to exist, not much of any neighborhood, I'd say.
The jingling of musical beads, a drum, wailing

somewhere in the background of the band,
as though its players were born playing.

I could not tell if you were wailing or singing,
clapping, stomping your feet in between

the music and the words of the music, and then
I became transformed, a skinny child, singing your

rhythms in a place overtaken by poverty and that
faraway fear of tomorrow, and Tubman, when

he brought you to town, I guess he never told you
about me or my friends; he never told you about

the poor squatters down Slipway. Me and my
friends, playing in the dirt that was our Monrovia,

in the hard dry poverty Tubman left us to ponder.
In our flip-flops, my friends and me, in someone's

parlor as old people played you, the hero, crying
for freedom. How could I know the reason you

wailed in my daytime and in my girl dreaming
at night, in the Bishop Brooks darkness?

Where was South Africa, anyway, I wanted to ask
someone, and what was it you said when your

voice cried out loud, singing, "*Thula, Mama, Thula?*"
One day, on TV, there you were with Tubman, you,

wearing your bubba, a jumper, pleated in the back,
and soon all of us girls were running all over

the place, wearing flamingo skirts and Mariam
Makeba bubbas like our mothers. You were the song

we sang, Mariam Makeba, the song worn around
our hearts and our backs, the song we cried,

and danced, and laughed to, despite us and the hard
times, and our shoes, we thought, were made

as hard as you at the 26th Day Dance. But little did
I know with my girl mind, how invincible the woman

was, Mother of Africa, mother of the freedom song
and the living dirge that could not be explained,

the voice of so many strings. In college, I found you
again, and knew why you would not go away.

But I found Soweto only after I discovered myself.

When Monrovia Rises

The city is not a crippled woman at all. This city
is not a blind man at a potholed roadside, his

cane, longer than his eye, waiting for coins to fall
into his bowl, in a land where all the coins were lost

at war. When Monrovia rises, the city rises with
a bang, and I, throwing off my damp beddings,

wake up with a soft prayer on my lips. Even God
in the Heavens knows how fragile this place is.

This city is not an egg or it would have long
emerged from its shell, a small fiery woman

with the legs of snakes. All day, boys younger
than history can remember, shout at one another

on a street corner near me about a country they
have never seen. Girls wearing old T-shirts speak

a new language, a corruption by that same ugly war.
You see, they have never seen better times.

Everyone here barricades themselves behind steel
doors, steel bars, and those who can afford also

have walls this high. Here, we're all afraid that one
of us may light a match and start the fire again

or maybe one among us may break into our home
and slash us all up not for our wealth, but for

the memories they still carry under angry eyelids.
Maybe God will come down one day without his boots.

Maybe someone will someday convince us that after
all the city was leveled, we are all the same after all,

same mother, same father, same root, same country,
all of us, branches and limbs of the same oak.

This Is the Real Leaving

This is the real leaving, and as I look around
this Pagos Island neighborhood, where we

used to think the world held its poles together
around us, I'm afraid of saying good-bye.

Here, the neighbor children cling and cling, their
eyes, uncertain of tomorrow. But children do not

always know that they are poor or wretched,
and cannot discern how their future will be

by what they eat or wear. They cannot
always see into tomorrow from where they live

or what degree of poverty they possess, or the
difference between what their neighbors own,

nor can they know how wealthy others are
by the material possessions, scattered around

a neighbor's yard. Maybe they wonder why.
Maybe they do not wonder. I walked in the door

yesterday, and emptied a fridge full of *torborgee*,
palm butter, fried fish, and so much good food

my son had left uneaten. They may never know
why I'm angry that there's food in my fridge

while others starve; today, the neighborhood
children had a feast; one feast, one big meal

today, but tomorrow, there will be nothing.
This is the real leaving, the detachment from

clinging things and people, and so often, I am so
broken, I become like a hard string, an angry

thing, baffled by this unevenness of a world
we are able to change. I wake up, and in my heart,

I am holding onto a child whose mother's protruding
abdomen was so alive, but today, upon my return,

they tell me the child died soon after birth, an
infant, born, already lacking blood, born in a shack.

How does the world expect an infant whose mother
has no blood to bring forth a child with blood

in its veins? This is the real leaving, a departure
from clinging things, forever imbedded in my heart.

To recover a world once lost is as hard as crossing
the stream of swampland between Paynesville

and me, the swamp behind my yard, the swampland
between the place where poverty ends and where

wealth begins. This is the real leaving, my child,
this is where we leave the shores to paddle afar,

but in paddling, we lose the shores, where we were
born to wade the deep waters our mothers could

not wade. And yet, in wading, we have to leave again.

BOOK II

Colliding Worlds

In My Dream

In my dream, I'm on the road, flying
somewhere, stranded at an airport.
I've lost my car or lost the keys
in my lost purse.
Or I'm in the airport security line
without my passport, a lone traveler
without a country.

So they want to know my country.
They want to know my place of birth.
They want to know the map that got me lost.
They want to know the name of those
who shattered my dream,
shattered my lost country.

So I say, I'm a woman looking for home,
displaced, a bag of useless goods
for my journey, a flip-flap, a ragged
bundle that only a refugee carries.
I'm the lost and unfound, from those
who did not come on boats,

those that did not come ticketed
in chains, those who did not fit in chains,
those, neither welcome by those who came
on boats nor in chains. I'm among
the newcomers, the new, newcomers.
Those who came, ticketed

not by plane tickets or train tickets.
Those who came, ticketed by live bullets,

grenades, and rocket missiles,
those, still bleeding from their sides,
those who found their way here
by crawling among the dead.

Sometimes, I Close My Eyes

Sometimes I see the world, scattered
in small brick shacks along the hillsides
far away in Colombia,

where it is only the poor, at the peak
of the mountains. Medellin, holding on
so the city can find rest.

Sometimes, I see the poor in my *Bai*,
shoeless and old, his teeth threatening
to leave him if he continued on,

and walking on barefoot, he looks ahead,
his eyes, not betraying the future, where
the children he's populated

the globe with will cradle him beneath
the soil, where we all go, poor or rich,
where we all go, if we believe in the grave.

Sometimes, it is just these children who
have emerged from a long war they never
saw; children, left along

the sewage drains, the same people who
brought on the war, now recapturing
the land as if the land could be captured.

Sometimes, the world is hazy, as if fog
were a thing for the artist's rough canvas.
Sometimes, the world is *Iyeeh's*

shattered water gourd, the one *Iyeeh* told
you not to drop, her world, shattered
but sometimes, this is the way of the world,

the simple, ordinary world, where things are
sometimes too ordinary to matter. Sometimes,
I close my eyes, so I don't have to see the world.

Sandy

LOVE SONG FOR THE HURRICANE WOMAN

Go away, Sandy, darling, go away.
The night is too long for a hurricane,
and the waters, dark and dreary.
A woman by herself is category 7 hurricane,
so where do they come from,
naming another hurricane after a woman?

Here, the winds are already twisting
the calendar in places where not even
fall can toss a leaf.
Fall is upon us, my love, and the wine
bottle has emptied itself of wanting.
Go, shut the blinds, my lover,
and let the winds dance, but do not
turn over the heart that has been lonely
so long, it is no longer a heart.

Here, night is irreparable, a torn garment,
the tear itself began from the hem.
I do not delight in good-byes, you know,
and I do not know that a woman
has to be a storm. Go away,
Sandy, and when the sun is up,
and when the ocean is calm, and when
the winds are still or when

you are no longer a storm, I will take
you at dawn. I do not know the language
of storms and I do not wish to know.

But if you speak of a long journey
somewhere in the dropping of leaves,
in the breaking of trees, the falling
of bridges a lover's feet need,
then I'll say, Sandy, my darling,
let your storm calm my heart.

Tsunami

A SONG FOR AN UNKNOWN YOUNG MAN

"Ah, this is how I will die," a young man cries.
Caught in the waves washing waves, car against

car, the rubble and the clean of water, all merging,
humans and their toys, gathered in one mighty

heap, catastrophe of catastrophes, ah, this world
has come to an end again, and so violently.

"Ah, this is how I will die," a small print that
each of us sees sometime before the dying itself

finally comes. As if in some kind of revolt, earth
has poured out its anger upon us again, so far away,

and yet the rubble and that helplessness revisits
us in our small comforts here in our own

make-believe world. Waves, mightier than waves
have gathered all the wealth of the cities into

one large heap; pile upon pile, houses sitting upon
other houses, cars upon cars upon houses,

where mighty highways fall as if in resignation.
Containers piled up as if they were crayons,

awaiting this same young man to draw up a new
world from a small boy's eyes. As if to make

some kind of metaphoric point or some kind
of philosophical statement not meant for today.

If only we could store all of this hard memory
onto a memory card or drive outside of memory.

Again, the earth has evicted us from what we
thought was our civilization. This kind of sorrow

would have made my *Iyeeh* stand in her open
doorway, arms, spread out or maybe, her two hands

upon her head, piling up all that grief upon
her bare head, and in tears, she'd stand there,

wailing, "But God, what did we not give you
or give you that you have brought this upon us?"

Or she would simply have stretched out her legs
on the *Mat*, *"Po-po wlee-oh, po-po-wlee-oh,"*

wailing, and villagers would come pouring into
her hut like rain. Today, I sit here, aging

in America as I wonder what another old woman,
her eyes watery and looking upon her new calamity,

this Japan, so vulnerable. This other woman,
wailing in a language only those familiar with

that sort of grief can know, and how is it that
a young man can come so close to death in such

a wise way, greeting death so kindly? But like
a survivor that he is, he must go on, having

brushed against death so unexpectedly without
letting go. But how does earth live on after this?

For My Children, Growing Up in America

Wishing you more than the sunshine,
          more than the trees, more than the hills rising
as if hills didn't only grow, but also talked and walked,
and had time for climbing hills themselves.

Wishing you all and more than you could ever wish
to hold in your hands. Wishing life were a bed
you could unmake and remake, covers
to roll under, lift off, or roll all over until sunrise.

Wishing you could stand along the old river
that still flows back at home, where the Atlantic
still carries its patience as a woman carries a newborn
on her back. A woman who knows that the navel
string is as tender as dewdrops in the Harmattan.

Wishing I could still hold you and keep you
and make you cry until all your eyes were free
again, the way you used to be free.
Wishing that the sun were not just up above,
something we could all keep for ourselves,

so when the clouds got too cloudy, we could
let out our own little sunshine. Wishing that the trees
I planted in my backyard in my early years were here.
Trees I dreamed my children would climb
and fall from, and then we would rush them to the car

to take them to the hospital right up the road.
Wishing they would be there for their cousins who

outnumber the grains of sand on the beaches
along Sinkor's shores. Wishing you, my darlings,
had grown up where the trees do not lose their color,

where color does not lose its brilliance, where
color is not the defining line, where today is before us
as if today were tomorrow, a never-ending day
of winding roads and deep footpaths, leading
us back to Cape Palmas.

You Wouldn't Let Me Adopt My Dog

A POEM FOR ADE-JUAH

"Mom, you wouldn't let me adopt a dog in my dream,"
my daughter tells me. "Really? Go back to your
dream, my child, and adopt that dog," I say.

Tend to it, humor it, take it to the vet, clip its toenails.
Give it antibiotics and let it run wild on our lawn.
Allow it to pull at the neighbors' flowers, let it dig
up their wooden fence, knock down other peoples'
flowerpots, give it a name, and let it
roll under your comforter. Let it eat out of your bowl.

Tell the dog that its grandmother loves it very much.
She loves it as long as it remains in the dream world
of uneven spaces, so improperly laid out,
the dreamer cannot bring back into the real world
what belongs to the dream world.
May your dog grow old and tired, beyond dog years,
and may it give birth to many dog babies
to help populate the dream universe.

I want to squat when I greet your dog,
and let it lick my ring finger clean.
I want your dog to linger upon my doorstep
while I stroke its head. I want to populate
your dream world with myself even as a dog
that I'm so afraid of lives and leaps.
Go back, my sweet Ade, and tell the dog how
welcome it is, no matter what kind of dog it is.

But let it know that my knees now hurt; my back
wants to give way after too many babies,
and last night, my hip began to send new signals
my way, as if I were a bag of electric waves,
trying to tell the world I'm done.
Tell your dog that I do not have the résumé
to tend an American dog. Tell him I am still
African, in the way that my mother woke up
each day, wondering where the food
for us children would come from.

Tell your dog that I love dogs, but I wonder
if the child somewhere in my home village had
a bowl of dry rice and palm oil to eat this morning.
Tell him my father still needs me to send money
to feed a house full of motherless children
who have taken to living with him after the war.
Tell the dog that if I become rich and famous,

I'll let you cross over the threshold of the dream
world, into the real and bring him home
to meet his new family, where his grandmother
stands over the kitchen sink, wet hands
and eyes, listening to Ade-Juah as if the things
that plague this world were not much
bigger than a dream, as if the life
of one small dog were larger than life.

When I Grow Up

When I grow up, I want to be my daughter
and go study abroad in Greece,
sit on a rocky cliff in Nafplio, overlooking
the Argolis Gulf, a dog by my side
in case I fall off the cliff.
And posting this photo,
my mom will be so terrified,
she'll send me more money
from her grave where she's been for so long,
her money has already changed citizenship.

When I grow up, I want to be the dog,
standing on a cliff in Nafplio,
overlooking the Argolis Gulf
next to a Grebo woman's daughter,
studying abroad in Greece.
and in the lovely girl's photo, I'll stand
in front of her, so if I fall, she'll jump
down that cliff and rescue me from
her grandmother, dead so long, she
has no money to send from a grave, where
her citizenship has become that of a dog's.

When I grow up, I'll be the rock
on a cliff overlooking the Argolis Gulf
in Greece, where a dog is studying abroad,
with a girl as his guide dog.
And when they stand on top of me,
I'll shoot photos to their moms, the dog's
and the daughter of a Grebo woman,
whose mother has been dead so long,
she's turned into a Greek goddess.

When I grow up, I'll be the Argolis Gulf,
having wound my way
from the Mediterranean, wet as mist,
in a city so old, it needs the daughter
of African immigrants to study abroad.
I'll become that old town,
where a Grebo woman, having grown up,
decided to become her daughter.
And when there's no longer the daughter
studying abroad, or a dog, or a cliff,
I'll be the Grebo woman, studying abroad.

The Inequality of Dogs

I am intrigued by dogs, by American dogs
by their powerless power, how my friend
cuddles her golden retriever on her sofa,
intrigued by the unevenness with which ·
we entreat a dog for a false bone,
for a toy someone manufactured
for the supposed pleasure of an American dog,
intrigued by our misunderstanding
that a dog needs us or needs to be our best
friend, or that a dog cares for our evening
walk. I am afraid to own an American dog.

It is a fact that a dog has no say
what kind of president we choose
nor can it be represented by its own kind
in any form. And yet, we keep them, strap them
in collars and belts, name them, strap them
at poles, cage them for their own safety,
by our own laws, or like Mitt Romney,
we tie them on the roof of a moving family
car, despite our own affluence or our laws.

And how I still think of that homeless
woman on a street corner in Medellin,
the city of poetry and poets, a city, versed
in turning decades of war years into poetry.
As the bus full of us poets winds its way
around the city, far into the suburb,
I look, and there she was, a woman and her dogs,
all scrawled on the bare pavement.
And I think, oh, the faithfulness of dogs.

But we know that a dog does not know tears
or how to make laughter or poetry.
There she was, long skirt, her bundles
of homeless possessions flanked about her
like possessions. A carefree corner
of a sidewalk, on the cold corner of a busy
street that takes us out of the city
into the suburbs, and there she sat, a woman
too rich in dogs to care about our rush hour,
speeding motorists, the dying evening,
the sun, setting so slowly,
its yellow was becoming red like fire, red,

like blood, red, like pain, the color of red,
red, the color of bloody warfare.
And there she was, her eight dogs, her riches;
her dogs, her poverty; her dogs, her one
lone question; her dogs, made homeless, despite
their unwillingness to be homeless.
And all of us, people, as if we too could be
somewhere on a street corner, collared
and tagged, all of us, someone's possessions.
Were they to ask her why they too
were sprawled at a street corner?

Were they to ask her why she gave them
nothing but an unclaimed street corner,
and what if she had answered with the same
question? And I remember, here as I sit
in what used to be my master bedroom
before the war, now a guest in my own home
country, Liberia, but a guest still, Congo Town,
Liberia, where in the war, dogs were more masters
than dogs, eating everything, including us.

Today, around me, the sound of private
generators droning hard, the new Liberia of new
poverty, privacy and violation of privacy
by noisy generators, barking, howling
dogs, and then, I remember the American dog
that needs an evening walk.

In Grebo country, our people tell the story
of how a dog became man's best friend.
They say the dog was a wolf or a wolf's
cousin or a dog-wolf. Then one dark, thundery,
rainy night, winds howling in the jungle,
so all the animals gathered and sent the dog
to go begging for a burning
chunk of firewood in town. When dog arrived
in town, the hut was so warm and man
was so kind, dog never returned to the jungles.
Today, when the wolf gets lonely, when
the night is stormy, you can hear the wolf
howling, "Gbay-oooh," calling out
for dog to bring the burning firewood.

But the idea of homeless Colombian dogs
and their owner versus the homeless
Liberian dogs made homeless by war versus
an American dog versus the new Liberian skinny,
hungry dog, the dog that has never seen war,
yet resembles wartime dogs, a metaphor for pain,
a dog, barking hard outside my window,
its muscled neck breaking from barking
at the gate of the rich. Don't get me wrong,
it is not the watchdog of the rich.

Instead, it belongs to the poor, the shack
owner, the one whose children will
not eat tomorrow. The Liberian dog versus
the American dog versus the Colombian dog,
and I wonder about the legend of a Grebo dog,
so faithful, it came to town to beg us humans
for a chunk of burning firewood.
And I wonder about the faithfulness of a dog,
not thinking that a burning chunk
of firewood could not survive
the heavy, rainy Grebo night.

Or maybe, but the legend did tell us children,
seated around that flaming fireplace in Gbaliade,
Jabbehland, our homestead, us children looking up
at Iyeeh, retelling this old, old story.
She did not tell us that this was the reason
dog stayed and became man's best friend.
She did not tell me I could not own
an American dog, but in the jungle,
when it is cold and stormy, the wolf cries,
"*Gbay-oooh, Gbay-oooh.*"

Medellin from My Hotel Room Balcony

Outside my hotel room window,
Medellin has awakened again this morning
to the honking of cars, the banging
of old creaking steel against steel,
the moving and moving of people, dragging
themselves against day and night,
steel against steel, world against world.

Somewhere in the din of the city,
we find ourselves, all poets, visiting not to see
the city, but to bring poetry to this country
of survivors, a people who know how the image
of a poem can hold back the war.

We have come not only to inhale their story
despite our own unending wars, despite
our own deep scars, despite our stories, despite
the scarred places from which we have
all come, armed not with bullets,
but with words more powerful than bullets.
They call us world poets, the International
Poetry Festival of Medellin.

This morning, a group of us walk
single file along the narrow shoulder
of a busy street from the Poetry Hotel.
A newspaper cameraman follows us between
the street repair crew and the moving crowd
to the city center for a camera shot
before setting us free.

We are the free ones, I tell myself, as we
wander the city as if in search of ourselves.

You will never know how the years are held
back decade after decade so the long war
will end, so the children will grow old,
waiting not to grow old, so mothers will go
to their graves, where death also speaks Spanish,
where their Spanish cries daily of lost lovers.
The children wait as if they, too,
have become mountains, the children,
growing and dying in their waiting.

Morocco, on the Way to London

Here is North Africa,
all sprawled, desert, empty spaces of heat,
crisp-cut dryness of earth, splitting.
As if the earth, on its own, decided
that giving up the ghosts of Africa through
cracked landscape was the thing to do.
As far as the eye can see, not wasteland,
but the grassless ground, as we land.

Next to me at Casablanca's airport gate,
a woman, draped in white linens, her hajib,
purer than a virgin on her first night upon
immaculate sheets, before the consummation.
The woman, old and spent, her smile,
fixed and twisted over the years,
over desert grass, overdone.

As if sarcasm alone were a pillar of salt
out of the human frame of Lot's wife.
As if to her, I were Lot's wife, I come
sleeveless, to unbury myself from the heat
wave that has made its way out of the oven
that is the city, into the humid airport
terminal, the air, trapped around us.

We are all parched, roasted, and done
by takeoff. Maybe London will unbake us
and soak us in its old raindrops of memory,
haunting a continent that now haunts
this old city. All the women here
walk as if alike, draped in fine linens,

no need to claim their own waistlines
but do they complain like me?

And the men, in tight T-shirts as if
out of a movie scene, content to be men,
holding on to the hands of linen-draped girls,
so hot, men have decided to keep them
wrapped up and packaged, not for the eyes
of others long before they were born.
But the aged woman next to my seat,

a wheelchair, to guide us against
the condemnation she could have rained
on us new Jezebels. So this is North Africa,
the very tip of this gigantic bulge
of a continent that is ours, our homeland
where the bulge tips toward sea.
Up the long stairway to the plane
from Liberia, a man, thin and refined,

already tanned and Moroccan, takes
my overnight, overweight bag from me,
up the stairs, and a boy in Casablanca airport
runs downstairs with three dollars, 100 degree heat,
a bottle of water to quench my thirst
not just for water, but for Africa.
To know this unknown continent,
so vast, so different and as real as steel.

He calls me "Sister," his Arabic-refined
English, broken like the soil and sand
outdoors, and mine, that has been so
lost, even my own countrymen
strain to understand which English

I now speak. This airport worker hands
to me my precious bottle of water,
smiling and I think, oh, Africa,

all bottled up in sun and heat and wars
and pain, where the ordinary language
remains pure, like a virgin, where
the ordinary person is the same from east
to west from south to north, as if this
did not happen to us. As if someone
did not so long ago separate us
by color and language of greed.

To Libya

FEBRUARY 2011

When all is finally said and done,
there will be masses of graves of masses,

broken glass of pierced people,
and the children dying or already dead.

Somewhere, on a side street, someone's hair,
forgotten after the clean-up.

Shreds of hair on pavement, the reminder.
      And the counting of those

taken away at night will not begin

      until we have already forgotten
who it was that was taken.

Sometimes I Wonder

Sometimes I wonder,
        do flies fall in love, take their lovers out?
Do they, like us, forget to keep a date?
And how does a dog show off its new coat?
Do dogs sit up at night and wonder about
their lover's paws, about the reason
there is a spot on their lover's tail?

Do lions cuddle their lovers at night when
it is cold and dreary?
        Where are the scientists, and should
I trust the judgment of a scientist?
Do scientists know what day it is
when their lover's birthday arrives?
Do scientists fall in love, and do they,
like a fly, sit upon their lover's lap
when it is cold and dreary?

How does an elephant show off its tusk?
How does a leopard know when
it is time to quit hunting
and return to sleep with the one it loves?
Do leopards understand how to love?
And, what does a termite do other than
breaking things down?
Do termites fall in love or do they
just cut and chip at things they did not build?

Do warlords fall in love? I mean, give
me a break, did Charles Taylor love all those
women they called his wives during our war?

How does a rebel, holding on to a gun,
holding on to a grenade, holding on to another
person's blood, holding on to a carved skull
of an enemy, find time to shut his eyes?
And how does a rebel cuddle his wife
when it is cold and dreary?

How does the one, fighting in the jungle
make time to think?
Do rebels really fall in love, or is it like the fly,
fleeting and passing, like a bullet?
How does the heart that wants to kill
its enemy cool off to make love?
Do flies really know it when a rebel, in a room
they're flying above, make time for a kiss?

Do people fall in love, I mean, really, do they,
like people, know how to cuddle when they
        cuddle a lover or is it something like a fly?
Do people really find the time to separate
the loves that boil inside of us,
so that one is for the mother, the other
for the son, and then, remembering that
                a mother is not a wife?
So how does a man separate his wife
from his mother, and seriously,
I'm not talking about sex.
Do men really fall in love?

Or is it like the love of flies and fleas
or of the bug and crawling things
and termites, eating away a day,
the lion, the wild beast, passing,
the keeper of prostitutes, for a day?
What is it they do?

The Deer on My Lawn

So, the deer, seeing the cold, new snow,
the slush, the late winter,
she, emerging out of old dry twigs,
fall's cruelty, the leaves of this world
having abandoned their place.
The deer strolls between dry branches,
and then quietly, she stops
in the middle of the road near my mailbox
as if to wait for the mail woman.
After all, yesterday was Veteran's Day.

I wonder as the deer stands there, staring
at the valley behind my rising deck,
overlooking the houses that have
so magically overtaken her forest
or does she just stand there, wondering
where she left her fawns,
wondering why all these structures
have so magically lined themselves

along these hills, and this road,
this black, hard road, this curving thing,
this unreliable hard pavement,
this unnamed thing she must cross
to get to the other side, this hard thing
that has taken so many others like her
away, this new world, erected
by these alien creatures.

Or, she thinks, this hard road,
so she stands there, waiting and waiting

to see if one of those moving structures
would come for her,
after all, the world as it once was,
was taken long ago. So she stands there,

until I take out my smartphone
that is not smart enough to capture
such a sacred moment, but the deer,
smarter than us, strolls away slowly,
not like a deer, but like the owner
of a long lost world.

Leaves Are Leaving Us Again

And the roads are littered.
And the flowers have given up.
And the cold of last night, sapping
every fiber of every life
out of old, old oaks, out of the blood
of both the birch and the maple,
sucking all life out of life.
The trees have decided they no longer
need leaves. Here, nothing is eternal,
nothing is real. Here, the birds know it.
The groundhogs know it,
and the squirrel and the bat,
even the crawling insects know this.
Fall is upon us again, my love,
fall has again tossed up its own earth.
Fall is upon us again, my darling.
It is time to quit like the leaves.
It is time to fall asleep.

BOOK III

World (Un)/Breakable

I Want to Be the Woman

I don't want to be the other woman.
Don't want to stay up nights
for the phone call.
Take your excuses and pour them
down some rusty drain
as from a wine bottle,
and kill yourself at dawn.

I want to stay the woman who stands
there, waiting,
so her husband's lies rest like dust
on the wind's shields of an old car.
I want to carry deep scars
of brokenness all my life,
like our mothers' mothers' mothers,
who did not learn how to kill
that old African polygamy,
but killed it anyway.

I am The Woman, the maker of the bed,
the unused love keeper, the breeder
of fine children, scarred
only by broken dreams in the broken places,
where our foremothers found company
with other women, and buried
their babies' naval strings with hopes
that someday, something would happen.
No, I am already The Woman,
Khade Wheh, headwife,
the home-keeper, *Khade*, the owner
of the afterbirth and the afterbirth pains,

Khade Wheh, the holder of hot pots,
the keeper of the homestead,
the fireplace holder,
the powerless, powerful African woman,
after the old paths
of lonely women, betrothed
too early to unknown, ugly men.
No, I am not looking for love.
This body is too old
for lovers to hang out in my dreams
or in my daydreaming.

Don't lie to me. I am too beautiful for you.
Don't fool yourself. I do not need love.
I do not think my Iyeeh knew love,
and, I used to hear her say
that love could not make a farm.
My *Iyeeh*, whose bare feet
grew thorns from walking back
and forth from farm to farm homestead,
from farm to town, from tilling the land
like a husbandless wife,

my *Iyeeh*, who entertained all
the small wives of an already blind husband,
my *Bai*, who was not too blind
to sleep with multiple wives,
but *Iyeeh* had only one husband despite
the crowd of wives
populating her marriage.
Yes, I want to be the villain
only to my husband. I want to ground
my last years under a cold blanket,
to guard my woman part

from your invasion.
I want to greet my ancestors, our mothers,
with this old piece of my brokenness.
Yes, I am *Khade Wheh*,
the mother of mothers.

This Morning

The morning after love dies, only a wet leaf
lingers near the doorway.
All night, storm and the trees wrestled,
torrential rains, pouring down like waves.
This morning, the red earth, wet and soaked
in grief, the kind of grief there is no sun
to dry. She stands in the doorway, staring,
as if a road were capable of unfolding
and refolding itself to the winds.
Maybe his heart will return to you, she thinks.
Maybe your heart will revisit his heart.
Somehow, you tell yourself it has ended.
Not the storm, not the winds,
but all the beatings and the pain.
This is not really love that has ended,
the solitary woman tells herself.
This is the pain and only the pain
that was supposed to be love that has ended.
One day, you will know it,
the difference between what love should
be and what you think love is.
In the meantime, the ground is hardening
and the weathered leaf, flying off to better
winds, so you must too, she says to herself.

When I Was a Girl

My stepmother used to say
"Shut up, Marie, shut up.
A woman should be quiet."
So I'd try shutting up,
one minute, two minutes, three,
but then, something inside my belly
began to rise up
like sourdough,
rising, rising, slowly, rising
something, tightening up

like a big knot, the kind
that ties up forest branches
as if something needed
knotting up for the trees
and the branches not to know
movement, not to know air,
not to know the freedom
a bird knows
and my belly would say
to me, my little tiny
fourteen-year-old stubbornness,

the kind that lets a stepchild
know she has power.
And before she knew it, sitting there
next to my huge stepmother,
her heaviness of heart and body
like the heaviness of slapping hands,
I'd remember what my pa told me.

"A woman shouldn't be
shut up, Marie."
And then, four minutes, I'd
begin talking again, talking
fast, talking fast,
carrying on like the pepper bird
in the Liberian dawn,
a bird, without business.
And the knot at my belly button
would loosen, and before
I could speak again, I'd hear her say,
"Shut up, Marie. Something
will shut you up someday."

And I'd look across from her,
sitting on a dented stool,
somewhere in our old kitchen,
a huge pot, boiling without
worry, and I'd stare
into her fine, mean eyes,
and I'd say, "Alright, Ma, Alright."
But before she swallowed
in satisfaction, I'd begin
chattering again, chattering
on with my friends, chattering
about the worries
of a fourteen-year-old stepchild.

I'm Afraid of Emptiness

Like yesterday, down the long corridor
to the cardiologist's office,
the walls, bare, pale, a long corridor,
as if this were intentional,
as if to remind those coming to him
they may soon walk across this gulf
to eternity, the empty walls, bare
as if the photographer's canvas has forbidden
the sort of photos at the main offices
to hang on these walls.

The emptiness, after you walk downstairs,
fall's dead leaves covering the lawn
and the school bus, gone,
the children, all grown and gone,
the clock's ticking itself to death, and there
you are in the kitchen, coffee,
the empty fields, where across the gulf
your neighbor's llamas roam and roam,
no children screaming, and the landscape
giving in to the ghost of emptiness.

And how I would hate to walk across
the desert alone, walking and walking on
hot sand, the emptiness,
as if trees were told long ago,
sand is not where they can exist.
I hate it when all the words from your lips
are bare of words,

where it seems you never learned that words
can stand as pillars when all is falling,
as if the poet did not need the concreteness
of words to exist.
I'm afraid of the emptiness of your being,
the shell of nothing that you have become.

Silence

In the quiet of my empty days, I discover
that dry leaves rustle and a river sighs.

The Atlantic rises and rolls and roars,
and when a lion is approaching,

one will hear its roaring in the distance.
Here, silence is a great divider

between what is and what should be,
between what is and what should not be.

Here, I can lay my life down on a flat bed
and tabulate all the crossroads I have survived.

But now, it is your absence that tells me
you were always gone. Suddenly, I recall

the cricket's persistent creaking, the deep
void of a dark village night, the moon, edging

into oblivion so the sun can rise on Tugbakeh.
The owl's loud call in a small distance,

playing with the night of nights as if again
I'm in my *Borbor's* house in *Gbaliahde*,

in the far jungles of Grebo country, where
the Jabbeh land is Jabbehland, where

silence is silenced, so I can believe for once
I'm with myself and for once,

I can discover that in this life, we can love
but once, that everything else is flawed

and crippled and nothing.

I Want Everything

How do you negotiate something you cannot see?
But the woman on the phone is laying out in minute

details, the outcome of so many years of her marriage.
Gate 11, Detroit Airport, such an odd number,

where a woman takes out all the ammunitions of voice
with calm precision. As if this were only a board

for flattening out donut dough. This phone call
is so serious, all of us passengers, seated at the gate

are invited to listen. This is a matter for divorce, all
the property, partitioned in small portions right here,

amid the airport's new carpeting, so hard, it feels
like stepping on steel, and the feet of already weary

passengers becoming brittle and sore, and the years
that knew nothing about her impending divorce

are poised for accounting. "Listen to me," she declares,
as if you could see her now at her kitchen sink, her

dress splattered with cheese and oil and the years.
A woman, already old enough to be sixty or seventy

or just fifty-nine. "Five hundred thousand dollars
in hard cash," she says. This woman is calm, her

voice so still, it has become a windless thing, as if
she'd already killed this man in her heart years ago.

She may have soiled many pillows many nights,
I imagine. She may have crashed many wine glasses

after the consolation of wine bottles, the comfort,
only temporary, but potent enough to wipe away

years indiscriminately. Maybe she'd laid it all out
years ago, waiting for the boy to grow up, for little

Jessica to find herself. Maybe she'd swallowed
hard during many hard nights. Maybe she'd waited

and grew tired of waiting. "Five hundred thousand,
upfront, the lakefront property, five thousand dollars

of alimony each month and the 401k, oh, I meant,"
she smiles, gazing out the window, eyes, cold, tearful.

Who is she married to? I shake my head. Outside
the gate, our plane waits for nothing. In a few minutes,

it will navigate the clouds, parting blue sky from
white puffy balls, slashing up clouds so the plane

can exhale, so its passengers can stay breathing.
But how do we negotiate what we cannot touch

or feel? "I want it all," she says into the kind ears
of a smartphone. "Listen to me," the stranger woman,

divorcing her husband from Detroit, declares.
Detroit, what a place on which to lay out the issues

long distance. "I want everything." Everything.

Finally, the Allergist

Finally, the allergist. Dark circles around his eyes.
Tiny hands. Something tells me he's been at this thing

so long, he has become steel and bricks. He wants
to know everything about my breathing. Everything.

I want to tell him that I have brought four children into
this world, one by one, my blood giving them flesh

so they would come out, head first. I wonder if I should
tell him how for several months now, my husband

has walked around the house, mute, as if with the legs
of flying ghosts, his feet, tapping softly, he has become

a cloud ball. I need to tell this allergist that it is not
just dust and mold a woman is allergic to, not just

falling leaves from fall's cruel cold that swells the chest
and fills a woman's lungs with slime gathered from

so long ago. I think I'll let him stop the poking of my
skin to listen as I tell him how standing at the altar,

a bride's dreams are as pure as dewdrops, that it is not
just the sparkling of her long bridal gown or the tears

in her eyes that are unsure. For why would a bride
weep at the altar if she did not know how someday, all

of these bright flowers she now beholds may someday
be dead, like her own dreams of what this life was to be?

Maybe I'll tell him that I am that bride, now aging
slowly, unlike other girls my age, but that my knees

hurt so bad, I'm already eighty in my knees. Maybe
I'll let this stranger simply poke my tired skin in silence,

searching for what makes a woman my age cough
and cough until she coughs up all the pain below her

belly button. Maybe he'll finally discover what ails
a woman like me after the onset of middle age,

after the children, after the landscape on which
we grounded our years has eroded, after the years.

I Dreamed

I dreamed you were a king of some place,
but the kingdom was lost in my dream.
So we gathered sticks in my dream
to build you a kingdom where you could sit
and pine and whine and make
the ocean foam with only your anger.

I dreamed you were a king of some place,
but the town had no name.
So, we lined up some ugly, crawling crabs
so they could be the people you ruled,
but after the black ugly creatures gathered
along the swamps somewhere,
they decided they did not want you
for their king.

I dreamed you were the king among the dead,
but the name of the gravesite lost
its place on the map.
The owner of the land did not pay his taxes
and lost the deed to the town's mayor.

So, those buried in your graveyard
rose up to declare you were no longer a king.
In my dream, you were unable to walk
or talk, so I wondered,
how was it you could not walk
if you were the same king my dream saw.

I dreamed you were the air in my dream.
So, I took some mosquito spray

and sprayed into you, and then you swallowed
yourself whole and became
the spray instead of the king my dream
worked so hard to make you.

On the Midnight Train

To sit and watch the way a passenger rises
from sleep, from a huddled position, ready

to possess the world with claws and teeth, despite
the moving superliner, is something to see.

From Pittsburgh, it's midnight, as the train drags
its way out, going west. The train, unyielding,

twisting us side to side, four o'clock in the morning,
the mad winds and the rain against windowed

darkness, baby, some devil's twisting the winds
in a boiling pot for tornadoes tonight. But folks

getting off in Toledo are packing up now.
The train's hooting, the sleeping towns, swaying

to the winds of things, passengers, shoving, pushing,
reaching for bags and shoes and blankets like

people on the move, like people who have lived
an entire century on the train, people who may never

know the way the other side of the tracks works.
Now, our car is emptying itself of those who,

not by will are train riders and bus riders. The girls
at the front of me have decided to do the whole

dress-up and dress-down thing right here in the aisles,
in full view, between delicate rows of sweatshirt

spaces, clothing tossed for hours to the abandonment
of floor. The woman on the other row across from

me is red-haired, freckled face, and plump.
Everyone here is heavy, but the red-haired has

strapped her crying infant to her chest. It is not out
of need of warmth or need of love for her unwilling

infant that she does this. It is not out of luxury, she
carries her already strong-willed child at her breast.

Right here, pants are rearranged on half-naked
buttocks, tattoos, reexamined, and the girl in front

of me turns to the other girl who is fast turning into
a tattoo museum, "Do you want to leave this here?"

I hear her say. Something too small for my eyes,
just inches away from me? She points to it the way

you point to a gun, the way you point to a machete
that's still red with the blood of your last murdered

victim. It is an egg, wide eyed, I tell myself on
the midnight train to Chicago. Since it takes both

of them to get this unknown thing from its hiding
place, the tattooed girl picks up the unknown

thing; the other girl unrolls an end of their blanket,
and the tattooed girl puts the thing in a fold while

the other rolls it the way a chef rolls an eggroll
before it hits oil and execution. They look at each

other and smile and then frown, a whole new world
rolling itself out before my untrained eyes, despite

my third eye, where a poet can remake an entire
world from just pieces of twigs. On the floor,

the red-haired and her baby are ready to depart
the train, but there's a parcel, not forgotten,

but left for us. A bag full of baby poop, left so
I can have something to gaze at, so I can have

something to write about. She knows, somehow,
that I have come a long way just for this.

Maybe she thinks I'm on a train to nowhere.
On my first train ride in ten years, a train ride

just for the sheer luxury of knowing sleeplessness.
"This is the last smoking stop," the agent's voice

drums out to us, and I wonder, "last smoking stop"?
I replay this in my head, turning around the idea

of a last smoking stop. As if a smoker, preparing
to die, needed a last smoke before the grave.

On an airplane, where my own world of seat-belted
folks sits like a bunch of coiled snakes, ready to bite,

ready to explode, there's no "last smoking stop" for us.
What is this, I ask myself. But everyone is filing out

again, everyone, dragging old duffle bags, leftover
food in plastic cans. Here, everything is so real, even

the ghetto finally emerges on us, though, not from
the woods, but from what we have come to call "city."

No pretenses, no overhanging clouds, no moving
winds to hide what is unreal from the real.

Here, everything is raw and hard like a question.
If you would pierce an arm tonight, you'd see blood,

real as the earth, unlike the programmed, portfolio
toting folks on my side of the railroad tracks.

First Class

I hate First Class. I hate the cold buttons
you have to press for all the "inconveniences"

you did not know at home. I hate the temporary
luxury, afraid to sit at the edge of my huge,

plush seating, among a bunch of big pocket folks
with their need for fine wines and beer, cheap

laughs, and all the luxuries life cannot afford.
Down the long aisles, there's rustling and talking

and loud laughing, where the coach class is free
to roam the plane like air bubbles, even though

they're forbidden to use the lavatory that belongs
only to the first class. Theirs is the real world of tight

spaces with no room for the leg to stretch itself.
But in first class, I'm the party crasher, longing

for a touch as real as stone. In coach class, a man
may hover over you, bump into you in return

for a smile, where a four-year-old kicks your old
back, screaming all night as her mother holds tightly

onto herself so she does not lose herself. In first
class, if you don't drink, you're wasting money,

girl, so, flight attendant, could you please get me
out of here, into a window seat among a bunch

of loud snoring regulars, in a small seat, where
three Irish men stand in the back of the Chinese

airliner, fifteen hours to Hong Kong, sipping wines
and laughing loud, where I can stumble upon them

with the freedom to ask if they are indeed Irish
or British or Australian, and in response, they

stare at me, asking if I'm the only one who does
not know that no other people on the globe

would stand at the back of a bumpy plane, holding
tightly to free wine unless they were Irish.

In coach class, I bump into old friends, where an
entire aisle is filled with Twenty-First-Century American

missionaries of the new order, chatting about their
journey to "fixing" the unfixable Africa, believing

this was what Jesus would do, that is, if Jesus would
have taken a plane instead of a boat in the rough seas.

This Is Facebook

On Facebook, someone adds me, someone deletes
me. Someone dies somewhere far out in India,
in a small crowded marketplace, in a small

village. Someone with a computer in a place
where there are no roads, befriends me.
He has a scarred face or heart or arm, but

I do not know. Someone posts a comment;
another erases theirs. I come up to my computer
in the dark of night, and another friend is on.

They say, "Hi." I say, "Hi." They may be a ghost
somewhere in Nigeria, writing from a dark
shrine of old gods and ancestors, twisting

and turning in their graves. They may be a drug
dealer somewhere next door, I do not know.
Someone says, "Hi." The photo he posts

has no hands. Has no face. Someone on my
friendship list is threatening to die. Someone
on my list will hang herself tonight.

In the morning, I'll see my friends list drop
down by one number, by two numbers, by three,
by who cares? This is facebook.

Faceless and nameless, all this is just numbers.
All the dark omens of the past, converging here
in this new spirituality of connected,

disconnected people. Someone adds me, someone
deletes me, like a word on a chalkboard.
I never knew there'd be a day when I could

be deleted, altogether, deleted. All my arms
and my skin and bones, deleted by an unknown
angel or criminal. How do I know?

What sort of friend deletes another, erases her
like a man, his first wife, for his second, his
second for his third, and on and on,

the deleting goes on. I say, "Hi." You say, "Hi."
I say, "Today the sun is up." You say, "Today
the sun is down." And all my facebook

friends say, "You go, girl." So I say, "Go where?
What have I done? Where should I go?"
So I delete someone. He has a mustache,

so I delete him. His face is covered. His hands
are hidden under his Facebook photo. Maybe
he has a gun. Maybe he thinks I have a gun.

But it's only facebook, my son tells me,
Facebook, I tell myself. Facebook.

A Room with a View

From my hospital room window, the city rises
through sky, steel city, three rivers, bridges,

broken and unbroken. A friend once told me
how this city has more bridges than any other

city, bridges so broken, they have become only
relics of the past. Outside my window, an old,

old city theater, where students from grade
schools stand in line for a visit, but my camera

lens are only for the homes on the far hill; homes,
I have heard, to come down, sliding when heavy

rains overwhelm the city, but again, they rise,
like towers, and their owners again repossess them.

This third day, fifth round of chemotherapy opens
slowly with rain, fog, clouds, so the windowpanes

in my photo reminds me that even a rainy day can
be beautiful as the beauty of hard times, the beauty

in the mystery of illness, the quiet of a hospital
room, when all you can do is reflect on the beauty

of your past life through raindrops against your
window glass, the beauty of homes against

the distant hills, bridge upon bridge, and the warmth
of my beddings, reminding me that I am still here.

Braiding Hair

Mercy, if it were a person, it would
be a soft cushion on which
the hair-braiding girl sits.

In six hours, your hair, parted from
        your large head, braided and done
    is just a few long braids.

Another six hours, and you're only
      halfway done. But your mamma
taught you how to sit forever.

And her mamma taught her too, how
   to stand forever. Your mammas
taught you how to be a girl.

Losing Hair

It's June 9, my sister Nanu's birthday,
and I am losing my hair.

The girl from Tugbakeh with all that hair,
her body so full of hair, hair down her

shoulders, hair, almost shutting her eyelids,
the girl that could have made a living selling

hair strands, now losing it all to the poisonous
venom of chemotherapy.

To keep life in my veins, they must purge
all life out of my veins. Life for life, hair

strand for hair strand, all the cells of my
body, crying out "don't kill me," but dying

still, so killer cells can drown themselves
in the war for life. I feel like I am again at war,

Liberia, in a refugee camp, where Peace Keepers
cannot keep peace without war, cannot save life

without the taking of life. To rescue us, they
shoot and kill, and all around, we lie dead.

The cells of my fine body, all dying, and if
there is a resurrection of dead cells, my cells

will again rise out of nothing, and all these
black strands of hair now falling with the gray

will know the solitude of losing, the solitude+
of the survivor's story, the solitude of cancer,

will know the absoluteness of fighting cancer.

Hair

So your hair has decided to leave you.
Be calm, this is a sacred moment.
So you're standing before the mirror,
horrified. Loads of long strands
have curled themselves for departure
from your head.
Soon, you will be as bald as a glass wall,
as bare as sidewalk, as a clay pot,
as jar, as marble, as solid as a globe,
your baldness, balder than bald,
but you are still a woman.
The despair they said you would know
has also left you.
After all, who needs hair
if they cannot live life?
After all, what is hair to a dead person
in a casket? After all,
how does the grave reconcile itself
to your long, dark hair
if not losing hair were a death sentence?
So, like the silly child that you are,
though grown and aging, a woman
after menopause, who under attack
by cancer, refuses to fall,
dance. Dance your way into life
again, into the beauty of the years
to come, into the days when your
grandchildren arrive to greet you,
dance with laughter, after all the pain
of chemo, the pain of hair
falling at your feet on your bathroom floor,

dance and make music come to life.
You will live through this.
And afterward, you will forget
you were even woman enough
to wonder about hair.
Dance and laugh, and let it fall.
Unless a seed falls to the ground and dies,
it cannot come to life, you were told.
So, dance into the new hair
that awaits you some day.

2014, My Mamma Never Knew You

When 2014 came in, we saw fireworks.
We saw wineglasses. We saw what we
always see on that first dark morning.
That life would be as kind to us as July rain,
as gentle as dew.
We saw a road that did not lead uphill
among gravel and thorns. We saw beauty,
the coming of spring and the birds,
flowers in bloom, not only on the branches
of trees, but in our eyes.
I saw it all, sitting on my living room
carpet, counting down.

I did not know that the year's counting down
was counting down for real.
Barely the year was in, and here came news
that somewhere inside my womb
was not a baby, was not fibroids, was not
anything you could just go in and slash out,
but inside that tender place, where only
warmth and love used to hold my babies
in place for nine months, in that beloved
and holy space was something as strange
as nothing my mother could have known.
So, when the doctor said "cancer,"
I thought she'd had too many wines.

So, like the warrior woman I was made to be,
I rose, upright, the way a farmer woman
grabs her hoe and her other tools around her
to capture the horrors of farming,

the way a newly widowed girl
calculates the farmwork only she must do.
I stood up and went to war
with this old Monster that has known only
strength over the decades at war with my fellow
women warriors. I went to battle,
only my heart as tool, only my strength, only
my bare fingers, my sense of humor, and my soul.

Somehow, I said to myself,
that if a woman can walk among the dead in one
of the world's bloodiest civil wars,
that same woman can meet and conquer
the Monster. I did not raise my white flag,
seeking to make peace with the Monster.
I did not lie down to die nor did I lay my tools down.
I went to war, the way all women have gone
to war bringing to life all the human
creatures earth has ever known.

After the womb was pulled out of place, its screws
uprooted and its loose parts, counted, the chain
that keeps life in place, unchained,
I cradled my face in my palms and wept hard,
that weeping a woman does when a child
is yanked out of her by nature.
So, I thought, well, it is all over now.
2014, I now saw the walls of my heart coming
back in place, as if the heart's walls could
of their own, fall and rise of their own.

Then comes May, flowers, here in my yard,
cool, misty winds, birds, returning
to present themselves, birds, affirming that

indeed, we can die and be rebirthed, May,
and I was now home, my womb, happily gone
and with no regrets, since a woman
who has already given her seeds
to the world in four living children, has no
need to wail over departed wombs and tubes,
and all that comes with the territory.
I met May, bruised, but alive, me, alive,
after the knife, after the scare of not waking up,
I held out my hand for May.

But somehow, in between the pain and the hope,
my father died. 2014, the year my mother
should have warned me about.
May, my father lay dead in a cold mortuary
in a faraway country that is not a faraway
country at all; my father, gone, and here I am,
fighting the Monster. Now, there was chemotherapy
at my door, and death news arrived on my phone
in a store parking lot, me, imprisoned,
not only in a car, but so far from that first

Po-po-wlee call, the coming of the *Nehwordeh*,
our townswomen, the daughters of the clan,
the gathering of the clan to open the door
so my father would cross over the threshold
into the other world.
I was not there when they laid *The Mat* down.

I like to take my days on pieces of splintered
wood. I like to take my life on slow ground,
when not just tears can heal my heart.

But it is only seven months, and now,
a new Monster, Ebola, like war, like cancer,
they call it Ebola, a plague, the untouchables
are the dying, but doctors and nurses die first.
How much death does it take for God to wake
up an evil people? How many plagues?
Why does a flower rise out of a petal at dawn
just to die before it unfolds itself?
Sometimes, I want to just walk until I walk
until I walk to a place where I was meant to go.
Sometimes, the road itself loses its footpath.
Sometimes, all we can do is to stand here
and fight the Monster.
Sometimes, I start my day with a prayer.
Maybe, this is all I was born to do.

CPSIA information can be obtained
at www.ICGtesting.com
Printed in the USA
LVOW08s2021250117
522162LV00001B/78/P